I0765679

10-DAYS AGING CHEAT SHEET: REVERSE ALL SIGNS OF AGING:

Natural Anti-Aging Foods and Drinks: Healing Superfoods to Stay Young Live Long

MELLISA DANIELS

iii

INTRODUCTION

Whether you're looking to turn back the hands of time so you can look and feel more youthful, or you are looking to improve mental clarity and memory, you'll want to **read every page of this special report** geared towards **highlighting the top anti-aging foods and supplements so you can live your best life.**

When it comes to looking, and feeling younger by staving off the signs of aging, there is nothing as effective and long-term than when you incorporate powerful anti-aging foods, supplements and nutrients into your diet.

There are very specific foods that are known to **boost** and **nurture** the production of collagen, as well as regenerate cells that help increase elasticity, making your skin look smooth and youthful.

Better yet, these foods and supplements go beyond simply reversing the effects of aging and improving the look and feel of your skin. They will also boost energy levels, improve your memory and focus and in many cases, they'll even help you fight off disease!

Are you ready to get on the path towards looking and feeling younger than you have in years?

Let's begin!

Contents

ACKNOWLEDGMENTS

Over the years, we have seen a number of clients come through our clinic doors, and after taking part in our program, the results that we saw after just a few days was impressive. I had been hesitant to put all these life changing lessons in a book, but it was Elsie, the day shift manager that actually set things up to have this book published and so I would like to thank her so dearly, and together with her, all the homeopathy teams, everyone who gave their valuable input that has enabled us to put together this book, Thank you all.

To Ellie, the scribe who did he best to always keep all the information we gathered safe, thank you so much for your dedication and a heart of resilience, that when everyone else would see no benefit, you always kept the small records, and it is those that have made this book a beauty of what it is today.

I thank my husband for the huge support he has accorded me, all the positive criticism that has kept the purpose of the book laser pinned and kept out all the unprofiting fables, it wouldn't have been this straight to the point without you, and our lovely children, who have never stopped to be an inspiration even in hard times. I thank you all.

FOREVER YOUNG

There may not be such a thing as a foundation of youth, but the foods and supplements featured in this chapter will quickly help you get on the path towards looking and feeling younger.

If *we are what we eat*, it's time to take a serious look at your diet and the type of foods you've been consuming that may contribute to lack of energy, brain fog, wrinkles and bad skin.

Instead of processed foods that leave your skin dry and wrinkled, stock up on these expert-recommended ingredients next time you are out grocery shopping and begin the transformation!

<u>Sesame Seeds</u>

Surprising? It shouldn't be. Sesame seeds are high in calcium and rich in many other minerals including magnesium, iron and fiber, - all of which support healthy bones.

Pineapples

Pineapple includes a powerful mineral called manganese which activates the prolidase enzyme, which helps with the formation and increased production of collagen.

Why does collagen matter so much?

An added boost of collagen production (that's created by the amino acid proline that comes from

pineapple) will give you an immediate improvement in skin strength and elasticity which will make you look youthful and toned.

Dark Chocolate

Not only is dark chocolate loaded with anti-aging benefits, but it's great as a replacement for sugary cravings if you're trying to cut carbs and lose weight.

Dark chocolate is packed with flavanols, which are known to increase blood flow to the skin which improves overall circulation.

As an added benefit, because of the flavanols found in dark chocolate, and their ability to absorb UV radiation, you'll be able to protect your skin from the damaging effects of sun exposure.

Blueberries

One of the top power berries of them all, blueberries contain more antioxidants than nearly any other fruit! Better yet, they also reduce skin damage caused by sun exposure.

But there's yet another reason to incorporate blueberries into your daily diet: they contain high

levels of Vitamin C which works to prevent wrinkles and

smooth fine lines.

Tip: Blueberries are also known to help protect your skin from emotional stress and even over exercising and the dark purple seeds from Concord grades are filled with polyphenols that will help keep your mind sharp.

Incorporate one-half cup of blueberries into your diet every day to prevent cell-structure damage and prevent the loss of firmness in your skin.

Pomegranate

It should come as no surprise that pomegranate is an essential fruit when it comes to anti-aging and softening your skin so that it looks and feels years younger.

Pomegranate is a top ingredient in many shakes, smoothies and vitamin-based drinks, as well as many anti-aging and weight loss recipes, because

of the high levels of ellagic acid and punicalagin, found in its seeds.

Ellagic acid is a compound that fights damage from free radicals, while punicalagin is a super nutrient that helps boost collagen production, and connective tissue - both of which will give your

skin a soft, plump and smooth look.

Tip: Try to incorporate more than pomegranate juice. Consider purchasing seeds that you can sprinkle into foods and recipes.

<u>Kale, Spinach or Swiss Chard</u>

When it comes to firming up that loose skin and minimizing wrinkles, take your pick between these three power foods.

These vital veggies include special phytonutrients that help protect your skin from sun damage, while fueling your body with antioxidant compounds.

Spinach is loaded with beta-carotene, a powerful nutrient that has been proven to improve overall skin elasticity.

Tip: Try to include 3-4 cups of kale, spinach or Swiss chard into your daily diet. Replace iceberg or romaine lettuce with spinach.

Swiss chard leaves, as well as Kale, are loaded with chlorophyll, a super nutrient that can block the effects of cancer-causing chemicals

LOVE THE SKIN YOU'RE IN

When it comes to reducing skin redness, fine lines and wrinkles, there are a handful of super-foods and nutrient-based supplements that you'll want to begin incorporating into your diet.

Let's take a closer look:

Top Foods for Reducing Fine Lines & Wrinkles

Watercress
Watercress is known to increase the circulation and delivery of nutrients and minerals throughout your body. This means improved oxygenation of the skin which will subsequently reduce fine lines and wrinkles.

Tip: Add a handful of watercress to a salad 3-4 times a week for maximum results.

Papaya
There are few superfoods quite as effective at boosting skin elasticity as papaya. They include a ton of antioxidants

as well as other important vitamins and minerals that will make your skin look smoother.

Some of these vitamins include: Vitamins A, C, E and K as well as magnesium, potassium and phosphorus.

Papaya is often found in skin masks and cosmetics because of its ability to help your body shed dead cells while working at helping to reduce inflammation.

Incorporating just 2-3 cups of papaya into your weekly diet will help you experience the many benefits of this power fruit.

Avocado

Known for its high levels of Vitamin A and B-complex, avocado is one of the best fruits for nourishing and moisturizing the skin. It's also a popular snack for those looking to lose weight as it is not only healthy but it will make you feel fuller for longer periods of time.

Top Foods for Increased Collagen Production

While your body is constantly at work, creating new collagen, somewhere around the age of 30-35 years old, collagen levels begin to taper off. Worse, the quality of collagen being produced is not as high as when you were younger.

This means that you need to take measures to incorporate foods and supplements into your life, as well as topical products if possible, that support and promote the production of new collagen on a regular basis.

Here are a few foods that will help restore and repair damaged

collagen while priming your body so you are also able to regenerate collagen.

Red Bell Peppers

These peppers are packed with antioxidants which are incredibly important when it comes to reversing the signs of aging. They contain high levels of Vitamin C as well as carotenoids, an incredibly powerful antioxidant.

The reason why antioxidants are so effective at looking and feeling younger is because they aid in skin repair, while also reducing inflammation and cleaning up reactive free radicals that can cause serious damage to our DNA.

Many antioxidants also work to stimulate the production of collagen which will help smooth out your skin while giving you a youthful glow.

You can find antioxidants in many different products including cosmetics, dietary supplements and even sunscreen.

Tip: Slice 1 cup of red bell peppers and dip them in Greek yogurt or hummus as a healthy, on-the-go snack.

Fish

Fish, such as salmon, haddock and tuna are loaded with omega-3 fatty acid which is imperative when it comes to regenerating collagen.

Red Veggies

We've already mentioned how red bell peppers are an effective way of boosting collagen levels but don't overlook all the other red veggies as many of them are equally as powerful including tomatoes and beets.

Red vegetables contain the potent antioxidant lycopene which not only works as a natural sunscreen, but it works towards increasing collagen levels in your body.

Soy

Quite simply, soy blocks the aging process. You can get your fill of soy from products like soy milk, tofu or cheese so do your best to work some of these foods into your diet.

If you're wondering why soy is so helpful at slowing down the aging process, it's because it contains genistein, a plant-based hormone that blocks MMP enzymes which age the skin

ANTI-AGING SECRET WEAPON

The truth is, the secret to reducing the signs of aging all come down to one thing: eating healthy.

Buying expensive creams or paying for treatments will only go so far and typically they are temporary which means you'd need to pay again and again just to maintain that youthful look.

However, with a healthy diet that includes foods rich in antioxidants and nutrients, you'll be able to enjoy a youthful look while feeling beautiful inside and out for many years to come.

Tips:

Avoid Inflammatory Foods
Cut out inflammatory foods such as fast foods as well as sugar, dairy and gluten. They all increase inflammation which speeds up the signs of aging. In addition, avoid processed foods whenever possible.

Stay Hydrated

Make sure you're drinking plenty of water in order to keep your skin looking smooth and healthy. The more hydrated your skin is, the healthier and younger you'll look.

Incorporate Omega Fatty Acids into your Diet

Fatty acids, such as flaxseeds, chia seeds, coconut oil and avocado are all great choices when it comes to keeping your skin hydrated.

Consume Protein

One of the reasons we get wrinkles is due to losing collage and elastin in our skin. One of the easiest ways to avoid losing elasticity is to consume proteins that contain amino acids. These powerful protein sources will help to repair skin damage and prevent premature aging.

You can find amino acids in foods like fish, grains, seeds and nuts. And you may be surprised to discover that tofu is yet another great source of amino acids.

Drink Rooibos Tea

Consuming this tea will fuel your body with important polyphenols which help protect your skin from premature aging, as well as excessive wrinkles. It's also a great alternative to coffee!

Tip: Replace your daily coffee with rooibos tea a few times a week. Coffee is known to dehydrate your skin so choosing rooibos tea as a substitute will help minimize that.

Focus on Citrus

Citrus fruits like oranges, tangerines, grapefruits and lemons are all rich in Vitamin C, but they also help amino acids transform into much-needed collagen.

Final Words

When it comes to reversing the signs of aging as well as minimizing unsightly wrinkles, red skin or fine lines, there are many ways you can do this without surgery.

Choosing a healthy diet is the most important decision you will make when it comes to looking and feeling younger on the inside out.

This special report has provided you with a starter list of foods and supplements to get you started, but you'll want to continue your research so you can incorporate as many super-foods and anti-aging protein and mineral sources into your diet as possible.

Here's to living your best life!

13

ABOUT THE AUTHOR

In the recent past, researchers have made breakthrough research discoveries on the field of ageing. Ageing is no longer an occurrence we wait for in fear, rather, we can keep or bodies young and strong.

We can control ageing y first understanding the key components that keep us youthful and strong.

Dr. Mellisa Daniels is a renowned naturopathic doctor and a leading authority on holistic health. Her unique approach combines natural and traditional medicine and homeopathy with nutritional biochemistry. She works to heal the underlying cause of disease, rather than suppress symptoms.

In this book Dr. Mellisa addresses the underlying cause of ageing, and focus to address those underlying reasons that will leave you feeling youthful.